THE KONGO KINGDOM

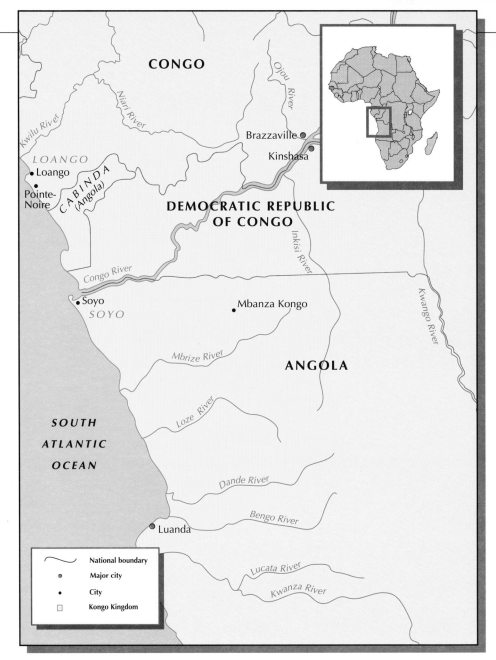

CONGO

Ojou River

Niari River

Kwilu River

Brazzaville

Kinshasa

LOANGO

Loango

Pointe-
Noire

CABINDA
(Angola)

DEMOCRATIC REPUBLIC
OF CONGO

Inkisi River

Kwango River

Congo River

Soyo

SOYO

Mbanza Kongo

Mbrize River

ANGOLA

Loze River

SOUTH

ATLANTIC

OCEAN

Dande River

Bengo River

Luanda

Lucata River

Kwanza River

National boundary

Major city

City

Kongo Kingdom

The Kongo Kingdom was one of the most powerful states in west central Africa from the late 1300s until 1655.

~African Civilizations~

THE KONGO KINGDOM

Manuel Jordán, Ph.D.

A First Book

Franklin Watts
A Division of Grolier Publishing
New York / London / Hong Kong / Sydney
Danbury, Connecticut

Cover photograph ©: Marc Felix.

Photographs copyright ©: Trip/W. Jacobs/The Viesti Collection, Inc.:
pp. 7, 8; courtesy of Manuel Jordán: pp. 11, 16, 28, 30; Mary Evans
Picture Library: p. 14; John Janzen: pp. 15, 36; The University of Iowa
Museum of Art, The Stanley Collection: pp. 19, 24, 32; from H. Capelo
and R. Ivens' *De Benguella às terras de Jacca*, Lisbon, 1881 (I:72): p. 21;
Ray Kerr: p. 35; Silver Burdett Ginn: p. 39; from O. Lopez and Filippo
Pigafetta's "Relations del Reame di Congo et delle Circonvicene Cen-
trale," Rome (Ed. Fac-Similé, preface de Rosa Capeans, Lisbon, 1949): p.
40; Library of Congress/ Corbis: pp. 43, 53, 56; Corbis: p. 44; Leonard de
Selva/Corbis: p. 47; Bojan Brecelj/Corbis: p. 49; Corbis-Bettman: p. 55.

Library of Congress Cataloging-in-Publication Data

Jordán, Manuel.
     The Kongo kingdom / Manuel Jordán. — 1st ed.
       p.   cm. — (A first book) (African civilizations)
     Includes bibliographical references and index.
     Summary: A survey of the history and culture of the Kongo
Kingdom in West and Central Africa that flourished from the late
1300s until 1655.
     ISBN 0-531-20282-8
     1. Kongo Kingdom—History—Juvenile literature. [1. Kongo
Kingdom—History.]   I. Title. II. Series. III. Series: African civiliza-
tions.
III. Series: African civilizations.
DT654.J67   1998
967.51'01—dc21   97-31290
                                                                CIP
                                                                AC

CONTENTS

INTRODUCTION 6

1 THE RISE OF THE KONGO KINGDOM 13

2 KONGO RELIGION 22

3 THE GOLDEN AGE 34

4 DECLINE OF THE KINGDOM 48

5 LEGACY 54

TIMELINE 58

GLOSSARY 59

FOR FURTHER READING 61

INDEX 62

INTRODUCTION

The Kongo Kingdom was one of the greatest states in west central Africa between the late 1300s and 1655. At the peak of its influence in the 1400s, the kingdom stretched from its center, in the north-western part of modern Angola, to areas south and east near the Kwango and Kwanza rivers. It also extended north beyond the Kwilu and Niari rivers in the present-day Democratic Republic of Congo (formerly Zaire).

The Kongo Kingdom was founded by the Kongo people, also known as Bakongo. They were a group of determined *immigrants* who traveled south into what is today Angola, crossing the Congo River. They established a kingdom with its capital at Mbanza Kongo. The first Kongo king, or *Mani Kongo*, controlled the trade routes that linked

The many rivers in the territory of the Kongo Kingdom enabled easy transport of people and trade goods.

the Atlantic coast with the interior in the Congo region. This enabled the Kongo Kingdom to become rich and powerful.

In 1483 Portuguese explorers first made contact with the Kongo Kingdom and the Mani Kongo.

The Kongo Kingdom covered vast territories, including densely forested areas.

Impressed with the well-organized kingdom, they soon sent missionaries, workers, and soldiers to support it and traded with the Mani Kongo. In return, the Kongo Kingdom provided the Portuguese with metals, ivory, and slaves.

By the early 1500s, the third Mani Kongo had

become a Christian. The kings of Portugal and the Kongo Kingdom regarded themselves as brothers. In agreement with the aims of the king of Portugal, the Mani Kongo encouraged his people to become Christian.

Many members of the Mani Kongo's court, however, wanted to preserve their traditional ways. They resisted the drive to Christianize their people and other aspects of Portuguese influence over Kongo affairs. This created severe conflicts within the kingdom, weakening it. The stability of the kingdom was further threatened by wars with neighboring peoples, who challenged the Kongo Kingdom's control of the profitable trade with the Portuguese.

One of the most important factors that weakened the Kongo Kingdom was the Portuguese themselves. As time went on, they made increasingly unreasonable demands for trade items, and they greatly expanded their slave raids in the region, even capturing Kongo people who were supposedly their allies.

In 1568, the Kongo Kingdom suffered a major defeat when the Jaga people invaded the kingdom and captured the capital. The Portuguese supported the Mani Kongo and eventually drove away the Jaga, but the political power of the kingdom declined greatly after the invasion. The Portuguese demanded that the Mani Kongo provide more goods and slaves to pay them for their military support.

The Kongo Kingdom managed to endure another century of internal divisions, conflicts with its neighbors, and Portuguese interference. But relations with Portugal deteriorated steadily, until the Portuguese fought and defeated the Kongo army in 1665. After the kingdom was defeated, it broke into smaller chiefdoms, each of which looked after its own interests.

The Kongo Kingdom had risen to power by uniting many peoples in the region into a state that provided a center of trade and political control. After the Portuguese came, Kongo kings tried to preserve and extend their gains by negotiating with the foreigners. They succeeded for two centuries, despite many difficulties and a deteriorating relationship with the Portuguese. By the seventeenth century, however, the presence of the Portuguese

A wooden Kongo sculpture with nails, known as an *nkisi nkondi*, or power figure. Kongo art is displayed in many museums throughout the world.

had changed the face of the region, particularly the systems of trade and politics. The final defeat of the Kongo Kingdom was the result of these changes. The Portuguese had grown more powerful. They realized that they no longer had to share power with the Kongo Kingdom; instead, they took what they wanted by force.

Although the Kongo Kingdom was destroyed, Kongo culture lived on, and it remains strong today. The Kongo and peoples who have been closely related to them throughout their history are still proud of their common culture, heritage, and past achievements. This sense of Kongo identity continues to play a significant role in contemporary Angola, where the Kongo Kingdom once flourished. Furthermore, most of the world's major art museums display examples of Kongo sculpture and other art objects. Through these examples of art, Kongo ideas are now shared with viewers worldwide.

THE RISE OF THE KONGO KINGDOM

The Kongo Kingdom was founded by Nimi a Lukeni, the son of a minor chief who lived in a territory north of the Congo River. It is said that he had the ambition to become a great king. In the late 1300s, Nimi a Lukeni and a group of followers traveled south across the mighty river. They conquered other peoples already settled there. Nimi a Lukeni established a capital and became the first Mani Kongo.

His capital, Mbanza Kongo, was built on a fertile plain atop a high plateau. Streams and rivers flowing below provided water to sustain the city and a means of transport. The elevation of the capital assured fresh air and cool breezes, provided

Mbanza Kongo sat on top of a plateau. This gave it a commanding view of the surrounding territory and helped defend the capital from invading enemies.

protection from invaders, and gave a sense of being in control of all the lands that it overlooked. Most important, however, Mbanza Kongo was strategically placed. Major trade routes, which linked areas north and south of the Congo River and linked the interior with the coast, all crossed at Mbanza Kongo. Nimi a Lukeni grew rich and powerful by controlling the trade routes. He forced traders to pay taxes.

SOCIETY

Before the arrival of the Portuguese, Kongo society was organized into three main classes: a *noble class*

Today, as in the past, rural Kongo women prepare food and cook meals for their families.

that controlled trade and governed the kingdom, a working class that provided labor and goods for trade, and slaves.

Among the working class, men built houses with mud brick walls and thatched roofs, harvested palm oil, made palm wine, hunted, and fished. Women farmed the land, tending and harvesting many crops, including millet, bananas, and, later, corn and manioc, which were introduced by the Portuguese in the 1500s. Women also prepared food for their families and took care of children.

Women in the kingdom's coastal areas produced salt by *evaporation* of ocean water, and harvested

One form of currency used in the Kongo Kingdom was *nzimbu*, seashells. The king controlled the supply of these shells, which were gathered on Luanda Island (above).

nzimbu, seashells, at the royal fisheries on Luanda Island. These shells were used as currency throughout the Kongo Kingdom and in other territories farther away. The Mani Kongo had absolute control of the fisheries and the currency.

Men pursued the arts of metalwork, woodcarving, and making cloth from the fibers of the raffia palm. Women were skilled potters and basket makers. This labor produced such necessary farming tools as axes and hoes and the pots and baskets needed to carry and store water and crops.

ADMINISTRATION

The working class lived in villages led by village leaders, or headmen. Most of the households in a village consisted of people related to the headman.

Slaves also lived in these villages and worked for the headmen. This early system of slavery in Africa was different from the system used in Europe and the Americas. In Kongo society, slaves were mainly war captives. They could eventually become absorbed into Kongo society and even occupy important positions.

Village heads had to answer to district leaders, who worked as administrators for the king and took care of legal matters. Most districts fell into one of six Kongo provinces—Mbamba, Mbata, Mpangu, Mpemba, Nsundi, and Soyo. Each province had a governor, who also served as one of the king's advisers.

THE KING

The Mani Kongo had the power to give or take away important positions and titles at will. Many court officials worked directly for him and took care of specific administrative duties from the capital. The king controlled court officials, provincial governors, district leaders, headmen, and the people.

Taxes were paid to the king in *nzimbu*, ivory, raffia cloth, slaves, and other luxury items. These taxes, known as *tribute*, came both from the king's *subjects* and from neighboring groups who acknowledged the authority of the powerful Mani Kongo. In turn, the king distributed some of the tribute to members of the noble class. This created a tribute economy: Valuable goods flowed to the king at the capital and then were distributed by him as rewards to nobles.

The king and his court used some of the tax money to pay the wages of their many court assistants. They also demonstrated their wealth and status by spending lavishly on ceremonies. Special occasions included reception of dignitaries, nomination of new nobles, weddings and funerals of nobles, and celebration of military victories and new diplomatic alliances.

Special types of art played an important role in Kongo public ceremonies, serving as symbols of status and prestige. Among the more important objects were ivory trumpets carved with royal

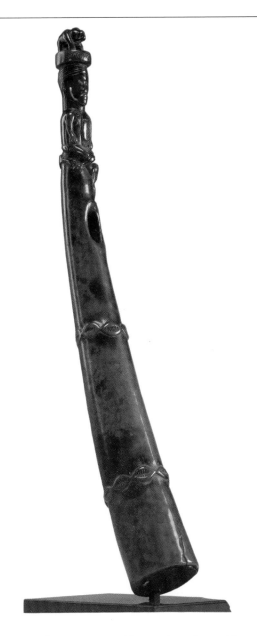

A Kongo ivory trumpet with a carving of a royal figure

figures, wooden scepters with inlaid metal decorations, flyswatters made from animal tails and with decorated handles, and skirts and caps made from raffia cloth with complex patterns.

Many of the Kongo art objects seen in museums today were made in the 1800s. It is not clear whether similar objects were made in earlier times. A Portuguese report from 1514 does mention, however, that the Kongo people used wooden "idols." This suggests that some types of wooden sculpture—particularly those representing royalty—were made early in the kingdom's history.

Male descendants of the Mani Kongo could aspire to become kings. Competition between potential *heirs* over who would next take the throne often created political rivalries in Kongo society and caused tension. The period after the death of a king was often unstable, as rival princes vied for the throne. Overall, however, the kingship worked well for the Kongo for centuries.

In many African countries today, kings, chiefs, and village heads still rule, although they share their traditional authority with other modern institutions of law and order. However, the hierarchy

Portuguese image of the burning of Kongo "idols"

of authority—from headman to chief or king—developed by the Kongo Kingdom and other African kingdoms still plays a role in modern government in many parts of Africa.

2 KONGO RELIGION

The Kongo people were so heavily influenced by Christianity after the arrival of the Portuguese that it is now difficult to detail earlier Kongo beliefs. Some evidence is available, however. Accounts dating from the early 1500s, written by the Portuguese and other European visitors, are one valuable source of information. Another source is Kongo oral history—accounts that have been passed by word of mouth from generation to generation. Some of these were even written down by European visitors centuries ago. Religious art, customs, and ceremonies that have continued for centuries are yet another source.

At the heart of Kongo religion, however, is a deep sense of the need for balance—between ancestors and the living, between humankind and nature.

SPIRITS

Kongo people traditionally believe in a Supreme Being or Creator, who is called Nzambi or Kalunga today. Nzambi is an extremely powerful spirit. Nzambi is so powerful, in fact, that he—or she, since some evidence suggests the Kongo people once viewed the Creator as female—is not involved in day-to-day human affairs.

Instead, the spirits of dead family members are believed to be powerful forces in the daily lives of their living relatives. The Kongo people remember and honor their ancestors through special religious ceremonies. The ceremonies establish and maintain a sense of balance and connection with the spirits of deceased ancestors.

The Kongo use *figurative sculpture* to honor the ancestors. This establishes a point of focus for the spirit. The ancestor is addressed often through the sculpture by prayers and invocations and by honoring his or her name. This ensures a good relationship

Phemba figures like the one pictured above were associated with Kongo funerary practices. The finely carved head of this *phemba* figure shows Kongo ideas of female beauty, such as full lips, round cheeks, and delicate chin.

with the ancestral spirits, who reward their descendants with health, children, successful harvests, and good fortune. If the ancestors are neglected, however, they are believed to punish the family with illness and misfortune.

Sculptural forms were created by Kongo artists to be used in *funerary* rituals and ceremonies. Stone or ceramic figures, called *mintadi*, were placed on the tombs of Kongo royalty as funerary monuments. Kongo artists also made finely carved mother-and-child wooden figures, called *phemba*. They represented the idea that the chief's *line of descent* continues even after the death of a member of the royal family.

NATURE SPIRITS

Other spirits recognized by the Kongo people include earth, sky, and water spirits that affect the environment. These extremely powerful spirits often behave unpredictably. They are shown special respect by the Kongo. As with the ancestors, this is done in an attempt to prevent the nature spirits from using their power to cause such natural disasters as drought or fatal lightning.

The following Kongo story illustrates the extraordinary powers and the unpredictability that the Kongo associate with nature spirits.

One day Mbumba the Rainbow left his home on earth to visit Nzazi the Lightning, Master of the Sky. Together they built a village in the heavens. Nzazi asked Mbumba to guard the village, but Mbumba the Rainbow refused and escaped by throwing himself into the water in the sky, sliding to earth, and hiding in a waterhole.

While he was hiding, a group of women came to the waterhole to fish and trapped Mbumba the Rainbow in their net. As the women began to haul in their net, Mbumba bit one of them on the finger so that she let go of the net. Mbumba transformed himself into a snake and, rising up menacingly, ordered the women to go away.

Mbumba decided to return to the sky. He discovered that Nzazi the Lightning, Master of the Sky, had gone out to strike six men dead on the earth. When Nzazi returned, Mbumba offered him a slave, but warned him that if he struck the slave he would suffer a great downpour of rain.

No sooner had Mbumba left than Nzazi the Lightning, Master of the Sky, became irritated with the slave and slapped him. The slave began to cry. Mbumba heard the crying far away on earth. Furious, he decided then and there to make good his threat. He set off to visit Phulu Bunzi, the Master of the Waters, to enlist his help in killing Nzazi. They put their heads together and made a plan.

Phulu Bunzi came out of the water dressed as a great chief and called Nzazi. When Nzazi the Lightning, Master of the Sky came, the Master of the Waters drenched him in a flood, quenching the fire of his lightning. Phulu Bunzi allowed Nzazi the Lightning to return to the sky after he had learned his lesson.

Phulu Bunzi stayed in Mbumba's village for a long time, until he found out that his own son had died during his absence. Phulu Bunzi blamed Mbumba the Rainbow for his son's death and eventually killed him. In this way the Master of the Waters showed his power over both Lightning and the Rainbow.

This photograph of a Kongo diviner, taken many years ago, shows him accompanied by a large *nkisi* that served as an aid in his work.

Elements of this story—such as the Rainbow serpent's biting the woman's finger and Lightning's traveling to earth to kill men—illustrate how vulnerable humans are to the unpredictable forces of nature. That is why nature spirits are recognized and honored.

DIVINERS

In traditional Kongo society, a diviner, or *nganga*, acts as a spiritual leader and a *mediator*, or go-between, a bridge between the human and the spiritual worlds. Diviners today use methods that are probably similar to those used during the early days of the Kongo Kingdom.

A diviner is aided by a personal ancestral spirit or other spirit that helps to uncover the cause of illness or misfortune in members of the community. A diviner therefore also acts as a traditional doctor or healer. Assisted by the guiding spirit, a diviner prescribes for a client the prayers and/or medicines necessary to cure a person or solve the problem. In traditional Kongo belief, almost all problems have a spiritual *component*. By consulting a diviner, an individual or a community can discover whether a particular conflict has been created by an angry ancestral spirit, an upset nature spirit, or a person with evil intentions who is practicing witchcraft.

Kongo diviners may use a variety of substances, objects, carved sculptures, and masks, all of which are believed to contain *supernatural* powers. Some of these aid communication with the diviner's ancestral spirit. Others embody powerful forms of spiritual force or energy. In the Kongo language they are called *nkisi* (n-KEE-see; plural *minkisi*), which means "spirit." The term is commonly used

On a postcard that is postmarked October 20, 1909, a Kongo diviner is shown with three *minkisi:* a wooden sculpture (right) and two bundles (left and center).

to refer to these powerful and magical objects and works of art.

MINKISI

Wooden sculptures of figures are a particularly powerful type of *nkisi*. These figures may represent either particular family ancestors or an ancestor that protects an entire community. Old Kongo *nkisi* figures, often called power figures, are now displayed in most of the world's important art museums.

The best-known and most dramatic type of *nkisi* figure is called an *nkisi nkondi*, meaning "spirit with nails." An *nkisi nkondi* figure is usually carved in the form of a human or a dog. When used by a diviner, the figure becomes the dwelling place of a specific ancestral spirit. A diviner drives a nail, blade, or similar sharp object into the wooden figure in order to attract the spirit's attention and enlist its help on behalf of a client.

The same procedure can be followed when two or more persons make an important agreement, contract, or treaty. By agreeing in the presence of the *nkisi*, the parties agree that if they break their promises they will have to face the anger—and the punishment—of the ancestral spirit that lives in the *nkisi*.

Once a particular problem has been solved with the help of the *nkisi*, or the agreement that was witnessed by the *nkisi* has been fulfilled, the diviner may pull out the blade or nail from the figure.

An *nkisi nkondi* becomes the dwelling place of an ancestral spirit when used by a Kongo diviner. The nails are driven into the figure to seek the help of the spirit.

Some diviners have said that the spirit itself "drops," or extracts, the nail or blade.

An *nkisi nkondi* in the form of a dog can be carved to represent a single dog or a two-headed dog with a head at either end of the body. Dogs are important to Kongo people because they serve as guards, or watchdogs. They are also believed to have the ability to see things that are invisible to humans. A double-headed dog is thought to be doubly watchful, guarding a person or a community in all directions against supernatural forces that may try to attack.

THE GOLDEN AGE

In 1482, messengers from the coast brought disturbing news to the ruling Mani Kongo, Nzinga a Kuwu, at the capital. Strange things had been seen out at sea. Some people described them as whales of a type never seen before. In fact, what they had observed were the first Portuguese *caravels*, or ships, to arrive in this part of Africa.

FIRST CONTACT

Before long, in 1483, the Portuguese landed. Their white skin was a cause of wonder, because the Kongo people associated whiteness with the spirit world: White was the color of the dead and their

Kongo healing mask used by a diviner. Masks made by Kongo and Kongo-related peoples often have whitened faces, because the color white is associated with the spirit world.

Loango, a coastal city north of the Congo River, became one of the major ports for early Portuguese-Kongo trade. An image of Loango published in the 1600s.

bones. In addition, the visitors had seemed to approach the coast from the west—the direction associated with the supernatural, with the "other world."

The Portuguese too were amazed. Led by Diogo Cão, they had anchored at a place called Mpinda in the *estuary* of the Congo River. They discovered that they were in Soyo, a province of a great kingdom whose king, the Mani Kongo, lived at Mbanza Kongo, a few days' journey from the coast.

Diogo Cão sent some of his men with Kongo guides to visit the capital. He arranged that he would sail farther south and then return to pick up his men. When he returned to Mpinda after sailing 700 miles (1,100 km) south, however, he did not find his men there as agreed. Uncertain about their fate, Diogo Cão took some Kongo men as *hostages* and set sail for Portugal.

In Lisbon, the capital of Portugal, the Portuguese king received the Kongo men with kindness and courtesy. At the end of two years in Portugal, the hostages had learned Portuguese and become Christians.

In 1485, Diogo Cão returned to Mpinda. Discovering that his men had not been harmed, he released his Kongo hostages, who greatly impressed the Mani Kongo with accounts of their time in Portugal. The Mani Kongo sent gifts of ivory, raffia cloth, and other goods to the coast as gifts for the king of Portugal. Diogo Cão departed for Portugal with these gifts. He left behind four Roman Catholic missionaries whose task it was to *convert* the Kongo to Christianity. In their place he took four Kongo nobles from Mpinda.

Two years later, Diogo Cão returned to Kongo, exchanging the Kongo nobles for the Portuguese missionaries. On the voyage back to Portugal, Diogo Cão died, but he had laid the foundation for a relationship of goodwill between the kingdoms of Portugal and Kongo.

PORTUGUESE INFLUENCE INCREASES

In 1491—a year before Christopher Columbus, the sailor from Genoa, Italy, set off on the first European voyage to the Americas—another Portuguese fleet arrived at the mouth of the Congo River. Commanded by Rui da Sousa, this fleet included missionaries, explorers, craftsmen, laborers, horses, tools, items used in Roman Catholic worship, and a variety of other goods that the Kongo people had never seen before.

One of the major missions of the Portuguese was to convert Kongo leaders to Roman Catholicism. The governor of Soyo agreed to be baptized. After receiving numerous gifts from the Portuguese, Mani Kongo Nzinga a Kuwu also embraced Roman Catholicism, together with many members of the royal family and other nobles. The king adopted the

In the early 1490s, Mani Kongo Nzinga a Kuwu was baptized Roman Catholic and took the Portuguese name João.

name of the Portuguese king, João (pronounced zhoh-OW; Portuguese for John). Nobles also took Portuguese names and titles. A church was built in the Kongo capital, which was renamed São Salvador.

TRADE

The Kongo Kingdom's wealth was based on trade. The ruling class immediately realized that the arrival of the Portuguese presented them with many new

Portuguese explorers traveled through the interior of the Kongo Kingdom on oxen and with the aid of local guides.

trading opportunities. They were eager to have the Portuguese, who were clearly rich and powerful, as business partners and military allies. The Portuguese could help the Kongo suppress rebellions in troublesome provinces—particularly Nsundi province. The Kongo believed the new alliance would enable them to increase their control of trade and territory.

Similarly, the Portuguese were delighted with the new avenues for trade that had opened up through their contact with the Kongo Kingdom. They needed a powerful African partner and ally to enable them to move about the region freely and explore new opportunities. At first, therefore, the relationship between the two kingdoms was mutually beneficial.

Even the pressure to become Roman Catholic that the Portuguese exerted on Kongo leaders may not, at first, have seemed excessive. The idea of worshiping one all-powerful God could have been interpreted as worshiping Nzambi, the Creator, who, until this time, had been seen as too powerful for humans to dare to pray to.

AFONSO I: THE CHRISTIAN KING

King João I and one of his sons, Mpanzu a Katima, are said to have abandoned Roman Catholicism and returned to the traditional Kongo religious beliefs between 1494 and 1506. This suggests that opposition to Roman Catholicism and Portuguese influence had begun by that time. Perhaps pressure from Kongo nobles forced the king and the prince to return to tradition.

Religion became the main issue in choosing who would succeed João. Mpanzu followed Kongo traditions. His brother Afonso, governor of the troublesome Nsundi province, favored Roman Catholicism and Portuguese influence in the kingdom.

In 1506, the two princes and their supporters

finally fought a battle near the capital. Afonso was victorious. His triumph was attributed to support from the Virgin Mary, who, it is said, appeared in a vision and blinded Mpanzu's forces with her divine light, and to the terrifying vision of Saint James riding on a white horse, which caused Mpanzu's soldiers to lose their nerve. Mpanzu was killed in the battle. Afonso became king and was recognized as such by King Manuel of Portugal.

Afonso used his victory to impress upon the people the power of the new religion of Roman Catholicism. He ordered his subjects to bring to the battleground for burning all the *minkisi* and other objects used in the old religion. He built a church in the capital, laying the foundation stone himself. He learned Portuguese and studied the Bible continually. He also created Roman Catholic schools and built churches throughout his kingdom.

King Manuel and Afonso I exchanged letters in the spirit of friendship and cooperation. Afonso I, a devout Roman Catholic, continued to work toward converting his people and frequently asked King Manuel, whom he called his brother, to send him more missionaries and teachers. Afonso also sent

The Mani Kongo receives a Portuguese delegation at the capital. He wears European clothes and is surrounded by luxurious fabrics. His subjects humble themselves before him as a sign of respect.

members of his family and the Kongo nobility to be educated in Portugal.

Roman Catholicism introduced new religious symbols to the Kongo—particularly crosses and *crucifixes* and figures of Jesus, the Virgin Mary, and saints. Kongo artists began to make wood or metal crosses and figures. For the first time, Kongo artists made images of the Creator, God or

Portuguese missionaries have been active in the Kongo region for more than five hundred years.

Nzambi. Before that time, Nzambi had been regarded as too sacred to be represented in art.

TENSIONS

During the reign of Afonso I, the kingdom entered into a full trade relationship with Portugal. The Kongo Kingdom sold the Portuguese slaves, copper, ivory (including tusks carved with figures and decorations), animal skins, and raffia cloth. It also provided the Portuguese with an entry into central Africa. In return, Portugal sent carpenters, masons, missionaries, weapons, and military support to the Kongo Kingdom. They also sent a wide variety of European goods and trinkets.

The Portuguese needed slaves to work the sugar plantations that they had established on the African islands of São Tomé (SOW-toh-MAY) and Príncipe (PREEN-see-peh) and in Brazil. Because the working and living conditions were inhumane, the slaves died in great numbers and had to be replaced frequently. As the European demand for sugar—a great luxury in those days—increased, the Portuguese expanded their plantations and their international sugar business. They needed ever more workers, and slaves became far more valuable to them than anything else the Kongo could offer. By 1516 the Kongo Kingdom was exporting four thousand slaves a year.

Afonso could not supply enough slaves without engaging in constant warfare against his neighbors to take captives. But raiding the kingdom's neighbors caused great political problems and damaged business relationships. Regional trade slowed because of resentments, and the kingdom's wealth and the king's authority were immediately threatened.

Although the Portuguese had sent soldiers and promises of military assistance to the Kongo, King Afonso often complained to the king of Portugal that these soldiers were uncooperative.

The Portuguese in the Kongo region came to realize that they did not have to conduct all their business through the Mani Kongo. They began to deal directly with Kongo nobles and neighboring peoples. This meant that the king no longer controlled the distribution of the trade items offered by the Portuguese, and could not reward his nobles with unique trade items. Since nobles could now obtain these tribute items—such as mirrors, umbrellas, and beads—directly from the Portuguese, their dependence on their own king and their loyalty toward him were reduced. Afonso complained to the king of Portugal that some of his subjects were becoming richer in these trade items than he himself.

The Portuguese also took the matter of the supply of slaves into their own hands. They began to kidnap Kongo people and conduct their own slave raids among neighboring peoples. Some Kongo nobles too began to deal in slaves for their own profit.

Kongo nobles began to obtain European items such as hats and umbrellas directly from Portuguese traders, bypassing and weakening King Afonso's control of trade and tribute items.

END OF THE GOLDEN AGE

Afonso I enriched and expanded the Kongo Kingdom. Although he and many other Kongo people embraced Roman Catholicism and Portuguese ways, many others opposed these changes and questioned the king's wisdom. Nonetheless, Afonso's reign, from 1506 to 1543, can be considered the golden age of Portuguese-Kongo relations. By the time of Afonso's death, however, those relations had deteriorated. Tensions had developed in the kingdom that would soon lead to its decline.

DECLINE OF THE KINGDOM

Many Portuguese saw their mission in the Kongo Kingdom as one of cooperation with a friendly nation. They showed goodwill and support. Others, however, aimed to make the kingdom an extension of Portugal. In this way they could *exploit* its rich natural resources and its population to satisfy Europe's ever-increasing demand for exotic goods and slaves for their plantations in the Americas. Many Portuguese in Kongo territory put personal gain ahead of cooperation between the two nations. Some Portuguese even *manipulated* Kongo politics to create war between provinces and with neighbors, because war provided the perfect opportunity for taking captives for the slave trade.

Many Portuguese traders in the Kongo Kingdom grew very rich—particularly from the slave trade. A wealthy Portuguese trader is carried in a palanquin, or sedan chair.

DIOGO I

After Afonso's death, Dom Pedro I was named Mani Kongo. But a people's revolt in the capital replaced him with Afonso's grandson, Diogo I, in 1545.

Diogo tried to control the Portuguese traders. He complained to Portugal about their behavior and the looting of *nzimbu* shells from the royal fisheries by Portuguese criminals.

Portuguese traders in São Tomé had developed a profitable business relationship with the Ndongo

Kingdom to the south of the Kongo Kingdom. They tried to ensure that Portugal traded with Ndongo rather than Kongo. Portuguese traders in Kongo, however, fought to prevent this. They forced Diogo to go to war with the Ndongo in 1556. The Kongo army was defeated, and by 1560 Portugal no longer traded exclusively with the Kongo Kingdom. Portuguese trade with the Ndongo and other peoples south of the Kongo eventually led to the founding of the Portuguese *colony* of Angola in 1575.

Diogo I fought and won other battles, but the political and economic power of his kingdom had greatly declined and continued to be challenged. Diogo also confronted problems with the Catholic Church because the Kongo nobility continued to marry several wives, including their own relatives—both of which were against church law.

When Diogo I died in 1561, disputes over who would succeed him broke out. The Portuguese became involved. Diogo's sons were killed by Diogo's brother, Bernardo, who became Mani Kongo. Bernardo also killed one of his brothers, causing him to fall into disfavor with the Portuguese Queen Catharina.

But Bernardo's reign was short; he was killed a few years later in a war with a neighboring people. His successor, Henrique I, suffered the same fate.

THE JAGA INVASION

In 1568 the new Mani Kongo, Alvare I, was defeated by the Jaga people. They occupied Kongo territory, destroyed São Salvador, and emptied the food storehouses. The Kongo Kingdom experienced famine. Portuguese traders took advantage of the situation by seizing some of the defeated Kongo—including nobles—as slaves for São Tomé.

Alvare I begged the Portuguese for help. The governor of São Tomé, Francisco de Gouvea, arrived with an army in 1571. It took them two years to expel the Jaga. Alvare I regained control of the kingdom, but he had to pay the Portuguese a great deal for the help they had provided. Portuguese influence was now stronger than ever, and the Kongo Kingdom was at its weakest.

Although Alvare I and his successors tried to rebuild the kingdom, its power had been destroyed. The problems and tensions that had surfaced under Afonso I grew worse and worse in the century following the Jaga invasion. The *nzimbu* currency lost its value, the profitable days of exclusive trade with Portugal were over, and the royal court and the Kongo nobility were increasingly corrupt, forcing the people to pay unreasonable taxes. More and more Kongo people were being kidnapped and sold as slaves, which added to a general feeling of uncertainty and distrust. The Kongo kings were no longer able to protect the interests of their people.

Several later Kongo kings tried desperately to ally themselves with the Dutch, who became rivals of the Portuguese in this part of Africa beginning in 1623. In 1648, however, a Portuguese fleet from Brazil defeated the Dutch, leaving the Kongo Kingdom in a weaker and more dangerous position than ever.

The Portuguese, who felt betrayed by the Kongo Kingdom's support of the Dutch, conquered the kingdom in 1655. This battle marked the end of the great kingdom established by Nimi a Lukeni in the late 1300s. New Kongo kings continued to be appointed, but the kingdom gradually disintegrated into several small groups led by minor chiefs.

II.
Scharmützel/den die Holländer verge=
bens mit den verrätherischen Portugalesern hielten.

Ls der Admiral/ der noch mit den Schiffen im Meer hielte/ solche Ver=
rätherey verstanden/ hatt er diese Schmach zurechen/120. wolgerüster Männer wid
die Portugaleser ans Landt gesetzet. Welche/ als sie ein gute Zeit mit einander ge=
scharmützelt vnd geschlagen/ haben die Holländer zwar den Feinden ihre Schantz
abzulauffen vnd abzutringen sich bemühet/ aber doch wegen Forcht grössers Scha=
dens/ endlich vnuerrichter Sachen widerumb abziehen müssen. Die Bedeutung der
Figur ist mit A. B. C. verzeichnet. A. sind die Schantzen der Portugaleser. B. ist
der Scharmützel den sie mit einander gethan. C. ist der Holländer Schantz/ welche sie bey einem fri=
schen Wasserfluß/zu Schutz vnd Vertheidigung deren/die die Schiff mit Wasser versehen/ auffge=
worffen vnd zugerichtet haben. D. Sind die Jndianische Männer vnd Weiber/ die in obberürter Jn=
sel wohnen. Der Mann ist ihrer Obersten einer/ welche gemeinlich mit einer Rondaschen vnd Spieß
gehen. Die Weiber gehen mit einem krummen Messer in der Hand/ vnd haben Paternoster vmb den
Halß/ die mit kleinen Creutzlein behänget sind/ denen sie durch Vberredung der Portugaleser grosse
Ehrerbietung bewiesen.

Contra=

The Dutch and the Portuguese were rivals in the trade with Africa. This image illustrates the competition between Dutch and Portuguese ships for control of trade in the colony of Angola.

5 LEGACY

Kongo people—and other peoples who were strongly influenced by the Kongo Kingdom—still proudly preserve many aspects of their heritage. In addition, Kongo culture was carried to the Americas through the slave trade. The Kongo captured and sold to the Portuguese neighboring peoples who held Kongo values, and many Kongo people were themselves sold into slavery when they were defeated in war. Kongo culture thus traveled across the Atlantic Ocean.

Today, Kongo names, words, songs, rhythms, symbols, and religious beliefs are preserved in the religious practices of the African *diaspora* in two

An estimated 2 million people from the Kongo region were enslaved, sold, and taken to work on plantations in the Americas, especially in Brazil and the Caribbean. The slaves carried their culture with them.

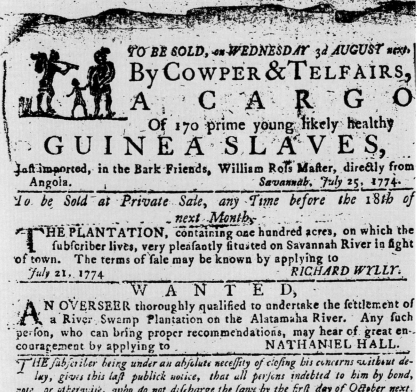

TO BE SOLD, on WEDNESDAY 3d AUGUST next,
By COWPER & TELFAIRS,
A CARGO
Of 170 prime young likely healthy
GUINEA SLAVES,
laft imported, in the Bark Friends, William Rofs Mafter, directly from
Angola. Savannah, July 25, 1774.

To be Sold at Private Sale, any Time before the 18th of
next Month,

THE PLANTATION, containing one hundred acres, on which the
fubfcriber lives, very pleafantly fituated on Savannah River in fight
of town. The terms of fale may be known by applying to
July 21, 1774 RICHARD WYLLY.

WANTED,
AN OVERSEER thoroughly qualified to undertake the fettlement of
a River Swamp Plantation on the Alatamaha River. Any fuch
perfon, who can bring proper recommendations, may hear of great en-
couragement by applying to NATHANIEL HALL.

THE fubfcriber being under an abfolute neceffity of clofing his concerns without de-
lay, gives this laft publick notice, that all perfons indebted to him by bond,
note or otherwife, who do not difcharge the fame by the firft day of October next,
will find their refpective obligations, &c in the hands of an Attorney to be fued for
without diftinction. It is hoped thofe concerned will avail themfelves of this notice.
PHILIP BOX.

RUN AWAY the 20th of May laft from John Forbes, Efq.'s plantation in St.
John's parifh, TWO NEGROES, named BILLY and QUAMINA, of the
Guinea Country, and fpeak good Englifh. Billy is lufty and well made, about 5 feet
10 or 11 inches high, of a black complection, has loft fome of his upper teeth, and
had on when he went away a white negroe cloth jacket and trowfers of the fame.
Quamina is ftout and well made, about 5 feet 10 or 11 inches high, very black,
has his country marks on his face, had on when he went away a jacket, trowfers
and robbin, of white negroe cloth. Whoever takes up faid Negroes, and deliver
them to me at the above plantation, or to the Warden of the Work-Houfe in Savannah, fhall receive a reward of 20s. befides what the law allows.
DAVIS AUSTIN.

Advertisement dated July 25, 1774 (top). The ad alerted potential buyers to an upcoming sale of slaves from the Portuguese colony of Angola. The sale took place in Savannah, Georgia, one of the thirteen British colonies in North America.

main forms: Candomblé (kahn-DOHM-blay) and Santería (sunt-uh-REE-a).

Candomblé is practiced mainly in Brazil, where Portuguese is spoken. Santería is common among some Spanish-speaking people from the Caribbean, particularly in Cuba, Puerto Rico, and the United States. For historically different reasons, both of these diaspora religions combine some traditional beliefs of the Kongo and the Yoruba people of Nigeria with symbols of the Roman Catholic Church. Kongo symbols and ideas are commonly found in the altars used by those who follow Candomblé and Santería. The Kongo version of the Christian cross is regarded as a particularly powerful sign.

Another important center of diaspora religion is the French-speaking country of Haiti, where the Vodou (voh-DOO) religion is followed. Vodou practice includes secret societies known as Kongo Societies and "power packets," or "power bundles," that are similar to Kongo *minkisi.*

The rich traditions of the Kongo Kingdom thus live on in both Africa and the Americas. Kongo art is now enjoyed by people all over the world.

TIMELINE

A.D. 1300s   Nimi a Lukeni becomes first Mani Kongo and founds the capital, Mbanza Kongo

1483   Diogo Cão and Portuguese explorers reach Kongo

1485   Cão returns to Kongo; he carries gifts back to Portugal

early 1490s   Rui da Sousa arrives at Kongo Kingdom; Mani Kongo Nzinga a Kuwu converts to Roman Catholicism and becomes João I; trade develops between Kongo Kingdom and Portugal

mid-1490s   João I rejects Roman Catholicism

1506   Afonso I becomes Mani Kongo; Kongo Kingdom has full trade relationship with Portugal

1543   Afonso I dies; Kongo-Portuguese relations deteriorate

1545   Dom Pedro I named Kongo king but dies; Diogo I becomes king

1556   Diogo I is forced to go to war against Ndongo neighbors

1560   Ndongo defeat Kongo; Portuguese trade with other peoples

1561   Diogo I dies

1568   Alvare I and Kongo army defeated by the Jaga people

1571   Portuguese military aid for Kongo arrives from São Tomé

1575   Portuguese found colony of Angola

1623   The Dutch begin to challenge Portuguese control over colony of Angola but are defeated in 1648

1655   Portuguese defeat Kongo Kingdom

GLOSSARY

caravel small ship with three masts and a broad bow

colony territory ruled by a distant country

component a part or aspect of something

convert to persuade a person to change his or her religious beliefs

crucifix cross with an image of Jesus Christ nailed to it

diaspora people who are moved from one part of the world to another, usually against their will, and their descendants

estuary place where an ocean meets a river and the waters intermingle

evaporation process by which liquids become heated and transform into gases that are usually invisible

exploit to use something to one's own advantage without concern for others

figurative sculpture Kongo sculpture that serves as a physical focal point for an ancestral spirit and for worship of an ancestral spirit

funerary having to do with a funeral

heir person who receives someone else's wealth or power when that person dies

hostages persons held prisoner as pledge that certain promises will be kept

immigrants persons who enter a country or region to establish permanent residence there

line of descent members of a family, especially rulers, descended from one person over generations

Mani Kongo king of the Kongo people

manipulate to change circumstances, usually with selfish or ill intent

mediator one who brings about agreement between disputing parties

nganga one who has the ability to intercede with the ancestral spirits and nature spirits

nkisi (plural *minkisi*) objects that assist in communication with the spirit world

noble class small group of people with high rank

nzimbu seashells used as currency by the Kongo people

subject person in a kingdom other than a member of the royalty or nobility

supernatural relating to a spirit or something beyond the physical world

tribute money or goods that a ruler requires to be paid by his subjects

FOR FURTHER READING

Mann, Kenny. *African Kingdoms of the Past: Kongo, Ndongo*. Parsippany, NJ: Dillon Press, 1996.

Okeke, Chika. *Kongo*. New York: Rosen Publishing Group, 1997.

FOR ADVANCED READERS

Bockie, Simon. *Death and the Invisible Powers: The World of Kongo Belief*. Bloomington: Indiana University Press, 1993.

Roy, Christopher. *Art and Life in Africa*. Iowa City, IA: University of Iowa Museum of Art, 1992.

WEB SITES

Due to the changeable nature of the Internet, sites appear and disappear very quickly. Internet addresses must be entered with capital and lowercase letters exactly as they appear.

Africa: The Art of a Continent—Central Africa: http://artnetweb.com/guggenheim/africa/central.html

Britannica Search—Kongo Kingdom: http://www.eb.com/cgi-bin/g?keywords=Kongo%20kingdom

Library of Congress—Federal Research Division—Country Studies: http://lcweb2.loc.gov/frd/cs/aotoc.html

INDEX

A
Afonso I, 41–47
Alvare I, 51–52
ancestors, honoring,
   23–25
Angola, 6, 12, 50
art, 12, 18–20, 22,
   30, 43–44, 57

C
Candomblé, 57
Cão, Diogo, 36–38
ceremonies, reli-
   gious, 22, 23
Christianity, 8–9,
   22, 37–39, 42
   opposition to, 41
   symbols of, 43–44
Congo, Democratic
   Republic of, 6
Congo River, 6,
   13–14, 36, 38
conversion, religious,
   37–38, 41
culture, Kongo, 12,
   54

D
da Sousa, Rui, 38
Diogo I, 49–50

dog, as spirit figure,
   31–33
Dutch rivalry, 52

H
hostages, Kongo, 37
houses, 15

I
"idols," wooden, 20
ivory, 8, 18, 37, 44
   trumpets, 18–20

J
Jaga people, 9–10
João, king of Portu-
   gal, 38–39
João I, Kongo king,
   38–39

K
Kongo Kingdom
   decline of, 10,
   48–57
   golden age of,
   34–47
   rise of, 13–21
Kongo people
   (Bakongo), 6,
   12, 25, 34, 54

M
Mani Kongo, 6–7,
   9–10, 13, 16,
   17–21, 34, 46
Mbanza Kongo
   (São Salvador),
   6, 13–14, 36,
   39, 51
Mbumba the
   Rainbow, 26–28
metals, 8, 16, 20
minkisi (spirits), 29
   30–33, 42
missionaries, 8, 37,
   38, 43, 45
Mpanzu a Katima,
   41, 42
Mpinda, 36–37

N
nature spirits, power
   of, 25–28
Ndongo Kingdom,
   49–50
nganga (diviner),
   28–29
Nimi a Lukeni,
   13–14, 52
nkisi (spirit), 29,
   30–33

nkisi nkondi (power figure), 31–32
noble class, 14–15, 18, 46
Nsundi province, 17, 40, 41
Nzambi (Creator), 23, 41, 44
Nzazi the Lightning, 26–28
nzimbu (seashell currency), 16, 18, 49, 52
Nzinga a Kuwu, 34, 38–39

O
oral history, 22

P
Phulu Bunzi, Master of Waters, 27
Portugal, king of, 9, 37, 39, 42
Portuguese arrival of, 34–37

exploitation by, 48–50
explorers, 7–8, 38
increasing influence of, 38–41
military support, 45, 46

R
raffia cloth, 16, 18, 20, 37
religion, traditional, 9, 22–33, 41, 54–57

S
salt, 15
Santería, 57
São Tomé, 45, 51
sculpture, 12, 20, 23–25, 29
slaves, 8, 10, 15, 17, 26–27, 44
Kongo people taken as, 52, 54
raids for, 9, 45–46

society, three-class, 14–17
Soyo province, 17, 36, 38
spirits, ancestral, 23–25, 29
succession, rivalry for, 20, 50–51

T
trade, 10–11, 39–41, 44–46, 50
routes, 6–7, 14
tribute, 18, 46

V
Vodou religion, 57

W
whiteness, as symbol, 34–36
women, role of, 15–16
woodcarving, 16, 20

ABOUT THE AUTHOR

Manuel Jordán is an art historian who specializes in the art and culture of central African peoples. He holds a B.A. in humanities from the University of Puerto Rico and an M.A. and Ph.D. in art history from the University of Iowa. Dr. Jordán has taught African, pre-Columbian, and Native American art at the University of Alabama–Birmingham and is the curator of the Arts of Africa and the Americas collection at the Birmingham Museum of Art. He has published a number of books and articles on African art and culture.